Christmas

by **Trudi Strain Trueit**

Reading Consultant: Nanci R. Vargus, Ed.D.

Marshall Cavendish
Benchmark
New York

Picture Words

 Christmas tree

 cookies

 gifts

 gingerbread house

house

lights

star

stockings

It is Christmas at our .

We put up a .

We put up a ⭐.

We hang .

We hang 🧦🧦🧦.

We make a .

We make .

We wrap .

We unwrap , too.
Merry Christmas!

Words to Know

Christmas (KRIS-mahs)
a holiday on December 25 that
celebrates the birth of Jesus Christ

unwrap (un-RAP)
to open

Find Out More

Books

Mckissack, Frederick L. Jr. and Lisa Berringer Mckissack. *Christmas Count and Celebrate*. Berkeley Heights, NJ: Enslow, 2009.

Prelutsky, Jack. *It's Christmas* (I Can Read Book 3). New York: HarperCollins, 2008.

Rustad, Martha E.H. *Christmas*. Mankato, MN: Capstone Press, 2009.

Websites

The History Channel: The History of Christmas
www.history.com/content/christmas

National Christmas Tree Association
www.christmastree.org/history.cfm

About the Author

Trudi Strain Trueit is the author of more than fifty fiction and nonfiction books for children, including *Kwanzaa* and *Hanukkah* in the Benchmark Rebus Holiday Fun series. Visit her website at **www.truditrueit.com**.

About the Reading Consultant

Nanci R. Vargus, Ed.D., wants all children to enjoy reading. She used to teach first grade. Now she works at the University of Indianapolis. Nanci helps young people become teachers. She enjoys spending Christmas with all her grandchildren.

Copyright © 2011 Marshall Cavendish Corporation

Published by Marshall Cavendish Benchmark
An imprint of Marshall Cavendish Corporation

Website: www.marshallcavendish.us

This publication represents the opinions and views of the author based on Trudi Strain Trueit's personal experience, knowledge, and research. The information in this book serves as a general guide only. The author and publisher have used their best efforts in preparing this book and disclaim liability rising directly and indirectly from the use and application of this book.

Other Marshall Cavendish Offices:
Marshall Cavendish International (Asia) Private Limited, 1 New Industrial Road, Singapore 536196 • Marshall Cavendish International (Thailand) Co Ltd. 253 Asoke, 12th Flr, Sukhumvit 21 Road, Klongtoey Nua, Wattana, Bangkok 10110, Thailand • Marshall Cavendish (Malaysia) Sdn Bhd, Times Subang, Lot 46, Subang Hi-Tech Industrial Park, Batu Tiga, 40000 Shah Alam, Selangor Darul Ehsan, Malaysia

Marshall Cavendish is a trademark of Times Publishing Limited

All websites were available and accurate when this book was sent to press.

Library of Congress Cataloging-in-Publication Data
Trueit, Trudi Strain.
Christmas / Trudi Strain Trueit.
        p. cm. — (Benchmark rebus. Holiday fun)
Includes bibliographical references.
Summary: " A simple introduction to Christmas using rebuses"—Provided by publisher.
ISBN 978-0-7614-4885-3
1. Christmas—Juvenile literature. 2. Rebuses—Juvenile literature. I. Title.
GT4985.5.T78 2009
394.2663—dc22
2009019058

Editor: Christina Gardeski
Publisher: Michelle Bisson
Art Director: Anahid Hamparian
Series Designer: Virginia Pope

Photo research by Connie Gardner
Cover photo by Think Stock/*Art Life Images*

The photographs in this book are used by permission and through the courtesy of:
Getty Images: p. 2 Lew Robertson, cookies; Yamanda Toro, gifts; Tetra Images, gingerbread house; p. 3 John and Lisa Merrill, house; Tooga, lights; Siede Preis, star; Thomas Northcut, stockings; p. 5 Jose Luis Pelaez; p. 9 Anderson Ross; p. 11 Jamie Grill; p. 17 Image Stock; p. 21 Ray Kachatorian. *PhotoEdit*: p. 7 Myrlee Ferguson. *Art Life Images*: p. 13 Jupiter Images. *Corbis*: pp. 15, 19 Ariel Skelley. *SuperStock*: p. 2 Comstock, Christmas tree.

Printed in Malaysia (T)
1 3 5 6 4 2